THE ORIGINALS

BEACH HOUSES TO FALL IN LOVE WITH

DEBORAH BIBBY

CONTENTS

FOREWORD

THE AUSTRALIAN BEACH REPRESENTED freedom for the early European settlers. For respite from their tough daily lives and the searing long summers of their adopted land, they sought the cooling relief of the Australian coastline. With little prior reference to life on a beach, they were enthralled by such a primal connection with nature: while their white skins turned rosy red and they experienced sunburn probably for the first time, they weren't daunted – they returned, seeking refuge under umbrellas and sun hats – and eventually sunscreens – while the urge for "a day at the beach" became more universal than watching the cricket.

The emergence of the beach shack was inevitable. Day visits overflowed into evenings and then the next day and the day after that. The early pioneers pitched tents under the stars and gathered around campfires to share food and stories. But that wasn't enough to satisfy this craving for the coast – its allure led ultimately to the emergence of water-side weekenders, somewhere to leave a footprint they could immediately revisit on their next break from the city. Just throw open the windows and air the bunk beds and you were ready for another seaside sojourn. Whether overnight, a weekend, a week or a month, this new breed of holiday-makers returned again and again to their seaside hideaways.

Often built by the resourceful owners themselves, these houses were initially very basic, simply a place to cook, wash and sleep, just a backdrop for bathing, lying in the sun, less structured daily routines and the sense of community fostered by freer and more open communication. The early beach house was little more than a glorified tent – and it often grew organically rather than by design – a jumble of rooms was added for overflow accommodation, inevitable for the steady stream of visiting relatives and family.

The resulting house typology reflected the lives of Australian settlers more accurately than any buildings inherited from Europe. In simple materials such as timber, fibro and corrugated iron, these buildings were unpretentious – they represented an innate response to place and a repositioning of priorities.

But Australians were not content with such a simple formula – they began to make their beach houses a home away from home by adding creature comforts, such as a fireplace as a gathering point, barbecues and outside showers. Communal sleep rooms meant the kids could recount stories into the night, while board games brought families together. And TVs and other modcons were left behind in the city – for a while, at least.

Each summer left its mark – mementos of that holiday were left to hang on the living-room wall, while more trees had been planted for precious shade – but, when it came to layout, informality and flexibility remained constant. Verandahs, open plan, shade structures, bunk rooms, water tanks and washhouses were all trademarks of those beach retreats.

The houses represented early settlers' response to the raw beauty of the Australian coastline. Nature was never far way – and they had no desire to exclude it or tame it. But then Australians' ongoing love affair with the beach shifted up a gear – they began to live full-time by the sea and coastal land became more valuable. Seaside towns became suburbs and convention crept into once-playful villages, while everything became more ordered and less spontaneous. Informality went out the window as the nature of the beach house shifted and increasingly reflected city values. The outdoors became the indoors with homes built to the boundary, apartment blocks replaced standalone homes, the ensuite became a must-have and discrete, private spaces became a formula for design.

While many beach homes fell prey to developers, fortunately many remain and are celebrated here. We can learn many lessons from them: functional simplicity, lifestyle enhancement, sensible scale, cost-efficiency, a relaxed, lived-in character that can't be made to order – and, perhaps most important of all in these times, their respect for nature and environmental sustainability.

The following examples of the traditional beach house, documented so beautifully in this book, look both back and forwards, embracing the past, while also offering new possibilities for today and into the future. The remarkable elegance of well-planned small spaces and the Aussie beach shack's amazing ability to adapt and change can offer valuable lessons for us all.

Peter Stutchbury, Architect

For my darling mum and son Jack,
thank you for all the love
and encouragement.

INTRODUCTION

FOR MOST OF US, HOME IS THE MOST IMPORTANT PLACE in the world, a refuge. All the homeowners in this book said, when first falling in love with their home, it was all about the kids – how they wanted them to grow up, what they wanted them to learn, feel and remember.

I've lived in our humble beach shack with my son, Jack, (until recently, as he's just moved out) for 20-plus years. It has been our haven during all the ups and downs of life and I chose it with him in mind. I wanted the experience and memories of the house to stay with him forever – from the banging of the flyscreen door to the doorstop that scrapes the timber floor, from the overflowing bookshelves to the squishy sofa that's seen tears, tantrums, loves and laughs, oh, and not forgetting those windows that rattle in the wind – all the emotions, memories, sounds, scents and good vibes of a happy house, well lived.

As a former editor of an interiors magazine, my passion for design, architecture and interiors is constant, but at the heart of this book is my love, respect and mindfulness for the quintessential beach house. I've watched too many disappear over the years. One demolition that broke my heart a few years ago was watching a beautiful pistachio-hued timber cottage on our beach being bulldozed – I cried that day. It was replaced with a three-storey, five-bedroom glass box completely out of proportion with the small beach. It prompted a desire to capture and share the stories of some incredible homes that have been saved and been lovingly restored.

So let me to introduce you to seven sublime beach houses as seen through the eyes of their intensely visual owners. They all have a story, a past. And their owners have embraced their original havens, in all their imperfections, their simplicity and their quirkiness, creating highly individual and, to quote homeowner Sarah Blair, "unsuburban" homes. To ignore the old is to fail to acknowledge the ties that connect us all. There is a movement to return to simplicity, whether retaining and restoring an older home or building a contemporary home in a way kinder to the environment. The more virtual the world and the quicker the pace, the more we are going to want to return to a crafted home. Your home is your story and it's an ongoing story, so make it last.

Deborah Bibby, Editor

THE LITTLE BLACK SHACK

A quiet place for contemplation and inspiration by the sea

PHOTOGRAPHY FELIX FOREST

PREVIOUS PAGE A recycled window frames Resolute Beach and Barrenjoey Headland, Pittwater, NSW. **ABOVE** Catching the sun and overlooking the bay in one of our favourite places to relax. **FOLLOWING PAGE** Weathered, timber-framed windows reflect the light over Pittwater. The crafted timber boat on the sill is from Antique General Store.

— — —

JAMIE & INGRID KWONG

Creative director & artist

WE WERE LUCKY ENOUGH to become the proud owners of the shack in 2013, but our relationship with it began many years before. More than 30 in fact.

In the mid '80s, I noticed the shack in a TV commercial and thought (even as a teenager), "What a cool place to live". From an early age, that humble little shack had a big impact on me. Because it was built in, around and out of stone and right on the water's edge, I assumed it was somewhere in the Mediterranean, somewhere on the other side of the world.

In my early 20s, I travelled to that other side of the world, backpacking with my partner, Ingrid, around the Greek Islands, French and Italian Rivieras and Spain. Humble little shacks made of stone dotted the shoreline everywhere we went – subconsciously, I was keeping an eye out for the one I'd seen in that TV commercial. I thought I would never see that shack again ... until a couple of years later, after travelling around Europe, living in London and getting married, we returned to Sydney.

One day, while out on the boat looking for Kingfish, we crossed Pittwater to try our luck at Mackerel Beach and, much to our surprise and delight, there right before us was The Shack. Incredibly, it looked just as I remembered it from that 1980s TV commercial. Small, crooked, humble. Perfect. We were in our mid 20s and, from that day on, made a point of going by the shack every time we were out on Pittwater - which was often. We fantasised about what life would be like there.

Then, one day on one of our many family boating trips in 2013, we passed by the shack just like every other time. Only this time, there was a 'For Sale' sign out the front.

We immediately rang the agent from our boat then jumped in our tender and made for the shore. After first setting foot inside the shack, and despite its rundown state, we were completely taken by the small collection of humble structures joined across the site in a crooked line. We loved how the buildings were all random shapes, sizes and angles and built around, in between and on top of large boulder formations. They had all been hand-built out of various materials and necessity over many years by fishermen wanting to shelter their families. We knew we had to buy it and rescue it to shelter our family, too.

So began an 18-month restoration to make good the 80-odd years of damage caused by the wind, the sun, the rain and the sea. Not to mention the termites.

...continued on page 30

SHACK
ADOBE
IN THE CITY
ALFRESCO
BY THE SEA
THE WAY WE LIVE
JODI PICOULT
Paullina Simons
Predator

we carefully pulled the broken, rickety, termite-ridden shack apart and put it back together as it was.

PREVIOUS PAGE The interior is curated with found objects, textures of wood, linen and leather, and celebrates the craftsmanship of the past. Painting of young girl, 'Happy Days', is by Nikki Bridger. Well-worn leather safari chairs from Lunatiques, Alexandria, NSW. We made the bookshelves from old second-hand planks collected over the years. **OPPOSITE** The interiors have a random feel, with their two-toned walls and the vintage painting, artist unknown, hung offcentre. **THIS PAGE** Our Little Black Shack, on the water's edge, is at one with its bushland setting.

Gone to
the
Beach

PREVIOUS PAGE We have recycled, upcycled or repurposed nearly everything in the shack, such as the vintage graters used as candle lights. The handmade wooden boats hung against the black rough-sawn-clad walls were from flea markets and we sourced the vintage harpoon from a local favourite treasure chest, Antique General Store, in North Narrabeen, NSW.
THIS PAGE The cupboard is made from timber repurposed from the ramp that we used to transfer building materials from the beach up to the shack. The window seat has been made even more inviting with textured linen cushions from Ici et Là, Botany, NSW.

THE WAY WE LIVE
BY THE SEA
IN THE CITY
ALFRESCO

TOP ROW Fittingly, the brass light at the front door, from online shop Edison Light Globes, was salvaged from a decommissioned ship; old fishing net from Eclectic Find, North Narrabeen, NSW; shell collection gathered from the beach at the bottom of the garden. **MIDDLE ROW** Garden taps repurposed over the kitchen sink; vintage painting sourced from eBay. **BOTTOM ROW** Sailing boat painting from Mick Mock; collected shells, corals, bottles and feathers sit on recycled shelves; we bought the enchanting mermaid clay sculpture in New Zealand 20 years ago. **OPPOSITE** Linen cushions from Ici et Là, wall light from Edison Light Globes and vintage boat from the local markets.

PREVIOUS PAGES We crafted the kitchen cupboards from the old original floorboards - well, the ones that the termites didn't eat! - then stained them with Porter's Paints Palm Beach Black stain. Basic brass cupboard and drawer handles from Bunnings. We gave them a bath in hydrochloric acid to remove the lacquer and shiny finish, then soaked them in sea water for a day or two. One of a series of photos taken by us on the ferry trip home, mounted in a frame that was a flea market find, as was the brass boat. **THIS PAGE** A bed we made ourselves. Softly crumpled linens in muted tones from In Bed, Paddington, NSW. Tapestry cushion a special find on a trip to Haleiwa, Hawaii. **OPPOSITE** Vintage deck chairs - the timber deck makes the most of the panoramic view. Deck chairs bought at a garage sale, while the upcycled tree stump doubles as a side table and sun umbrella stand.

We had one ambition – to positively influence
our environment and our guests, one couple,
one weekend at a time.

...continued from page 13

Lovers of second-hand things (the older the better), repurposing and recycling, we were determined that our efforts to make a home would make as little an impact on the environment as possible.

So, with the help of an incredible, young, environmentally friendly French builder named Jerome (of course), and a string of his international traveller mates, we carefully pulled the broken, rickety, termite-ridden shack apart and put it back together as it was. Using sustainable techniques and recycled or repurposed materials (where possible), we took our time and did things properly so it would last another 100 years.

Once the shack was rebuilt and weatherproofed, we filled it with our many pre-loved and much-loved finds gathered during 30 years of travels all over Australia and the world. Handy on the tools ourselves, if we didn't already own something or couldn't find it second-hand, inspired by the fishermen before us, we made it ourselves from materials that had been locally salvaged and recycled or gathered from the bush and the beach at our doorstep.

Because the shack was in such a bad state when we bought it, our first night there was not until it was restored, 18 months later. It was so worth the wait. After showering outside, cooking outside and reading by the open fire, we went to bed early and woke to the sunrise and the sound of the waves lapping on the shore below. We went for an early morning swim off the private beach at the bottom of the garden stairs and confessed to each other that we never wanted to leave.

As small as it was, and as big as our children were growing, we realised we had created our forever home. The sense of calm and appreciation we felt being surrounded by such a private and pristine environment also made us feel very protective over it.

...continued on page 42

PREVIOUS PAGE The king-size bed, handmade from salvaged timber, sits high enough for us to take in ever-changing sea views. **OPPOSITE** The vintage chair was found on the side of the road and reupholstered in a light blue Sunbrella fabric that teams perfectly with a half-painted wall in rich indigo blue. The '70s seascape painting, artist unknown, was from Mick Mock. **FOLLOWING PAGE** An old dresser, wicker chair, washed-up beach bottles and a vintage painting from Mick Mock decorate the guest room.

PREVIOUS PAGE The pizza oven and outdoor kitchen, new additions to the shack, have become the perfect place to cook and eat all year round. **ABOVE** Under a cross made of driftwood collected on the beach, guests can slip between blue linens from In Bed, Paddington, NSW. Tapestry cushion found on a trip to Haleiwa, Hawaii. **OPPOSITE** A rustic dresser from Elements I Love, Byron Bay, NSW, was converted into a vanity. Brass garden taps bought from Bunnings.

TOP ROW Old ropes, hard to come by, are handy for everyday use; still life by our friend and frequent visitor, Linda Barripp; the doors were built from leftover floorboards. It was hard enough getting the wood here, the last thing we wanted to do was take it back! **MIDDLE ROW** Vintage umbrella in sunshine hues; nautical flotsam and jetsam washed up on the shore. **BOTTOM ROW** The book selection instils a sense of adventure, while sea urchin shells match a bleached-white table; camping rugs are perfect for cool nights; split, barn-style doors let the breeze in and keep native animals out. **OPPOSITE** Writing desk, shell desk lamp gathered from markets. Vintage painting from Mick Mock.

…continued from page 30

We decided that first morning that we had to spend more time here than just on weekends. We had to make the shack our permanent home. However, with kids in school and the shack being accessible by boat only, we decided it was more practical to wait until the kids had all graduated and were old enough to come and go on their own. Fin, our youngest, wasn't due to finish high school for another seven years!

Unable to spend every weekend there and encouraged by friends and family who, like us, said they felt so much more in tune with and appreciative of nature and the environment while staying at the shack, we made the tough decision to open up our private shack to guests, in the hope they would feel what we felt. We had one ambition - to positively influence our environment and our guests, one couple, one weekend at a time.

It soon emerged the shack was not only what we needed, it was just what a lot of other people needed, too. A great antidote from the everyday stresses and excesses of modern life and work, here there are no shops, no roads and no cars. The shack is a true escape in every sense of the word. You find yourself falling in rhythm with the sun, the moon and the tides and enjoying the simple things in life. Like showering outside and catching, harvesting and cooking your own food over fire. Reading books, relaxing in a hammock, going to bed early and waking up early (without an alarm), swimming or sitting in the shade of a tree to cool down, or lighting a fire to warm up. And gazing out to sea through any one of the 14 recycled windows, instead of staring at a screen. Here we also watch the sun rise and set, the moon rise, thunderstorms approach and rainbows form, instead of the TV. We have no computer games or pay TV, but we have fishing rods, crab traps, kayaks, an extensive book library, a deck of cards, board games, a guitar and each other's company.

Until we're able to live here full time, we'd love to encourage more people to feel the same way about the planet as we do. If our sustainable little shack can positively influence others to care for the environment, as it has us, we'd be really happy. Judging by the wonderful feedback we've received so far, The Little Black Shack is doing just that.

PREVIOUS PAGE The hand-crafted clay mermaid was bought 20 years ago in New Zealand. **OPPOSITE** The stone terrace, shaded by a full frangipani tree, is the perfect place to pause and gaze out to Pittwater and Barrenjoey Headland. The stump table was upcycled from a neighbour's fallen tree.

WATERVIEW

Originally landfall for a sea captain, this home is now an idyllic family hideaway overlooking a wonderfully mercurial southern ocean

PHOTOGRAPHY SHARYN CAIRNS

HOBART

PREVIOUS PAGE Texture tantalises in this collection of ceramics and found objects in the living room, some of which were washed up on the beach below Waterview. **ABOVE** Past meets future – since the 1840s, Captain Kelly's weatherboard cottage has surveyed the wild and uncompromising landscape, where we always feel completely cut off from the world. **OPPOSITE** I am an incorrigible collector of special treasures. **FOLLOWING PAGE** Old and new narratives weave together – the large ceramic kitchen bowl on the living room credenza was unearthed from an abandoned ruin in Piedmont, Italy.

— — —

JOHN & SUSAN WARDLE

Architect & interior designer

IN 2002, MY WIFE SUSAN AND I travelled to Bruny Island, off Tasmania's southeast coast, and were captivated by its untamed beauty. And we fell in love with Waterview, this historic farming property. It had been on the market for five years at a time of great recession in rural Tasmania, but we saw it as an opportunity to restore and invest in something that would last. And the farm would be an antidote to our hectic lives in Melbourne.

Our priority was to remediate the land - building would come later. We began planting and simply getting to know our surrounds, 440 hectares of a working sheep farm. We set up a conservation reserve, placing over a third of the property in a covenant, to protect native vegetation and habitats, and help regenerate the land.

Built by harbourmaster and Antarctic explorer Captain Kelly in the 1840s, the original weatherboard cottage with wide verandah and pitched roof had fallen into disrepair. But what began as simple exercise in renovation became a historic and personal undertaking, to reveal the cottage's original character, while creating contemporary living spaces for family life. The cottage was complemented by the Shearers Quarters in 2012. Both were designed in response to the topography, the site's history, the existing working buildings and as a form of farmhouse typology.

Many details within the architectural vocabulary of Captain Kelly's Cottage are references to its locality and its history. We were fortunate enough to know an architectural historian, John Matthews, who set about unearthing stories of the original craftsmen and the various building techniques employed during the cottage's construction. It was built by many hands - from traditionally trained carpenters to shipbuilders and whale crew carpenters on the whaling off-season. The cottage had been extended and added to by farming families over the years, and, during demolition, these additions were selectively removed from the original shell.

I am endlessly enthralled by the stories of the past, and when they intersect with other more recent histories, they take on yet another level of appeal. Not only did we wish to make the cottage more habitable, but we were given the opportunity to thread the story of the Kelly family and the cottage's subsequent owners through the rebuild. It wasn't a process we could have anticipated from the outset.

Susan and I feel more connected to the cottage and its history, now this process has ended. There are constant reminders of the forebears of this home and our stories sit alongside them now, in conversation I like to think. Custodians of the property, we hope future generations take great interest in the tales of this land.

PREVIOUS PAGE The view from the living room to the remote bay has the dreamy luminous quality of an ancient landscape. Armchairs Ercol and Patricia Urquiola, chair Hans Wegner.
OPPOSITE All joinery, floors, walls and ceilings were crafted from Tasmanian oak, sourced directly from a single mill. The self-designed bespoke chair melts into the wall.
FOLLOWING PAGE New and old parts of the house sit in harmony with each other, gazing out to the rugged landscape and the everchanging Tasman Sea.

PREVIOUS PAGE Offering texture and warm sheen, bronze scalloped handmade INAX Yousai tiles, from Japan, are laid into a custom coffee table designed by myself. Layered antique rugs in muted natural hues and tactile patterned cushions add softness and a subtle counterpoint to the predominant timber palette. Golden light plays onto the barn-style shutters and pitched timber-clad ceiling. **ABOVE** Grouped objets d'art from our travels near and far engage with 'Small & Large Plain Series' etchings, 2003, by Philip Hunter. **OPPOSITE** Bronze, burnished tones and textures of the INAX Yohen Border finger mosaics reach for the ceiling and complement the brickwork in a bathroom.

PREVIOUS PAGE A beguiling view from the living room, the heart of the cottage, through the cruciform window and out to a grove of ancient walnut and mulberry trees. **OPPOSITE** Portuguese fabric covers the cushions on a window seat looking out to the firepit, which is made from an ancient cauldron, while the seats are reclaimed pier timbers. Both are spots to gather or simply daydream and enjoy the ocean vista.

OPPOSITE The verdigris swirl of seaweed in the ocean currents, captured from the cliff edge. **FOLLOWING PAGES** A backdrop for the new: paint layers stripped back in the main bedroom reveal the original patinaed tongue-and-groove cladding. Burel textiles from Portugal, indigo and cotton print curtains made by Maku Textiles in Calcutta. Paintings above the bed, 'Untitled 6202', 2006, by Julia Ritson, with Fijian chook basket below. Carved head from Bali.

1928
-1905
23

There are constant reminders of the forebears of this home and our stories sit alongside them now, in conversation I like to think.

PREVIOUS PAGES Stepping back in time in one of the bedrooms, where stripped layers of paint reveal news clippings and wallpaper from another era; a Parisian nude, artist unknown, is totally at home on a tongue-and-groove, colonial-style bedroom wall. **OPPOSITE** A timber folly screen and seat terminate the original wraparound verandah, channelling the view from the courtyard to the expansive ocean beyond. **FOLLOWING PAGES** The pounding waves of the Tasman Sea are constant reminders of how wild and wayward this piece of coastline can be.

GYPSY CREEK

A quirky creation in the Byron Bay hinterland overflows with a beachy, happy vibe

PHOTOGRAPHY SHARYN CAIRNS

ABOVE I am both an interior designer and gypsy at heart. **PREVIOUS PAGE** A mantel curated with treasures, an oversized brass safety pin and postcard of my Citroën 2CV. One of my own paintings hangs over the mantel. **FOLLOWING PAGE** A living room styled with honest pieces. The Spanish chair, by Danish designer Børge Mogensen, hugs a nook, while two squishy armchairs, called "the most comfortable armchairs in the world" by their manufacturer Maker & Son, fill the space. Big log side table by 'Twiggy' Greg Hatton, a favourite designer of mine. Painting by door a vintage find, artist unknown. The rest hunted out with my restless eye.

— — —

LOUELLA BOITEL-GILL

Interior designer

THERE'S SOMETHING ABOUT THE BYRON HINTERLAND in northern NSW, Australia, that transports me back to the rolling green fields of England, the tree-tunnelled winding country lanes and the greenness of it all. Except that is, for the fact that the Byron hinterland tumbles down to the most beautiful ocean beaches, is connected strongly with the water and is a little bit warmer than Blighty!

When I started looking for a house, I had no intention of buying anywhere but Sydney, but on the last day of a week-long stay in Byron I spotted a little Queenslander open for inspection and it was just too sweet not to look at. As I walked up the front steps, I knew this was it – the energy of the house had cast its spell on me.

This gorgeous little gem was presented for sale by Jan, an elegant ex-model, Miss Bondi 1957, no less. Jan had owned this cottage for 15 years and was struggling with the idea of leaving it and all her memories behind. It was only her age that was forcing the decision, and she was keen for someone to buy it who would nurture the house, not tear it down.

I got back home and recounted the story of this amazing woman to my good friend, Josh, who asked, "Is there a gypsy caravan in the back garden?" My response? "Errrrrm, yup. You know her?" It turns out that Jan was his old family friend and he and his family used to stay in the gypsy caravan when it was on her previous property. She had moved it from there and attached it to the deck at the back of the house to use as a spare room. Who would have thought?

So, when I told Jan what I wanted to do with the house and the connection, she felt the right person had come along and she was finally okay with selling. She has since popped in and is thrilled with the changes we've made and can't believe all the things we've held onto - she was very happy.

Everything about Gypsy Creek fell into place with ease. It hadn't been overly modernised, it had been cared for sensitively and with love and it still retained so much original character - it just needed a little update. The front steps ran crookedly sideways across the front of the house and were in dire need of repair. The first thing we did was build wider steps and run them straight, creating a strong, welcoming entryway and a beautiful extra area to sit in the afternoon sun. The main house has two bedrooms that work off the main living area and Jan had opened up the first bedroom with wide sliding barn doors, which works perfectly to make the

...continued on page 89

GYPSET STYLE
ASSOULINE
GYPSET TRAVEL
ASSOULINE
RICHARD LONG MIRAGE

PREVIOUS PAGES In the living room, Oregon-pine shelves hold curated finds gathered from around the world; Eames dining chairs in the sunroom are made super comfy with sheepskin throws while an oversized cotton pendant, from Society Inc, adds presence and a wonderful luminosity after the sun goes down. **THIS PAGE** You can only smile on arrival, as the most beautiful blue barn-style front door announces the colour palette of the house and leads your eye into the guest bedroom and through to the ensuite. Beds dressed in nostalgic linens by Society of Wanderers, wardrobe handles replaced with rope and sliding door pulls are Stone Hooks by Normann Copenhagen.

ABOVE An old trolley re-emerges as a rustic vanity, complete with bespoke copper taps. The Merchant basin is from Slabshapers, Byron Bay, NSW. **OPPOSITE** The ensuite with zinc bathtub, old sheep shearers bench as a vanity and stone bowl wash basin all lend a wonderfully bohemian air, in tune with my home's Byron location.

...continued from page 79
space feel larger. All we did was replace the handles on the cupboards with rope and add a pair of stone handles to the sliding doors.

Both bedrooms had sunrooms that ran off them and the old verandahs had been closed in with multiple classic Queensland windows installed above the timber walls to let in a little light. I turned both sunrooms into bathrooms, so each bedroom has its own bathroom, both complete with old zinc bath, one with a tiled shower. Not finished yet, the bathroom at the front of the house had old double glass doors out to the corner of the verandah, with another set of latticed double doors closing it off from the front verandah. This proved the perfect spot for a beach shower, tiled with the most amazing blue encaustic tiles. I obsessed over the rich colour.

The main thing we did structurally was pull out the kitchen, which included pulling out three pillared wall sections to open up the space. It meant adding a beam to span the roof, which automatically gave rise to the obligatory rope swing. Very important to have a rope swing in the kitchen! The new kitchen is one simple Oregon-pine bench with under-counter appliances the whole length, pull-drawer fridges and dishwasher, and a freestanding range. A crazy old heavy industrial workbench is another benchtop with drawers. It's an old piece from Belgium that I loved, but it had a decent-sized price tag. When I worked out how much joinery would cost though to do the same thing, the price tag didn't seem so bad!

The island bench is also the kitchen table. I designed it at bench height for stools and it has a lovely round Belfast sink dropped into it with exposed copper plumbing. I worked with a great plumber, who was happy to play at making taps and wastes - it was like a Meccano workshop.

The gypsy caravan only had one bunk, so we pulled out the wall section underneath, where the horse's bum would have been, and opened it up, rebuilding the bunk a bit deeper and adding a bunk underneath. When I looked at the opened space from the doorway, I realised we had to keep it open, and add a window. It was magical looking straight through to the garden outside.

Working on this house, by nurturing the character it already had and injecting further life into it with loads of vintage bits and pieces, has been so special. There's something about the way it makes you feel when you open the top half of the barn door and, with a chai in hand, look out over the street to the cafes and shops. It's a house that people drop into, wave at as they go by, a house that makes you feel calm, a friendly house. It's a house with a creek and rainforest at the back door, an ocean down the hill and ever-changing abundant wildlife. Sometimes it feels like they'll all move in too!

We all think we have far more control over this life of ours than we actually do, but things find us more than the other way around. When something is meant to be, there's no getting away from it. Gypsy Creek found us and we're very grateful. Our job is to look after her, just as she will look after us.

OPPOSITE An original zinc bathtub, with bespoke copper taps, is blissfully positioned under a bank of windows, where we can enjoy fresh air and views into the surrounding rainforest as we soak. **FOLLOWING PAGE** The homely and vibrant kitchen, with that must-have swing, Lale Rustic Milking Bar Stools from Inartisan and Love tea towel, hung as wall art, by Rachel Castle. Oregon-pine benchtops and kitchen table designed by myself. The industrial-style yellow pendant adds a pop of sunshine and instantly makes me smile.

The main thing we did structurally was pulling out the kitchen which included pulling out three pillared wall sections to open the space up. It meant adding a beam to span the roof, which automatically and obviously gave rise to the obligatory rope swing. Very important to have a rope swing in the kitchen. ☺

LOVE

3 4 5 6 7 8 MADE IN 9 ENGLAND 10 11 12 13 14 15 16

18 19 20 21 22 23 24 25 26 27 28 29 30 31

5

PREVIOUS PAGES An old pharmacy cabinet has been re-prescribed as shelving for family treasures; in the main bedroom, a flag from Pony Rider keeps watch over the bed and two industrial pendants serve as bedside lights, while a Babar the elephant vintage poster adds whimsy. Artwork, right, by Rachel Castle. **OPPOSITE** I was eager to retain the exuberant ceiling art adorning the gypsy caravan – I have further accentuated it with layers of vibrant bedlinen from The Society of Wanderers. **FOLLOWING PAGE** The exotic gypsy caravan, painted in colour Dulux 'Mildura' low VOC Taubmans paint, has become one with the forest.

SUNTRAP

A yellow shuttered haven on a clifftop, bathed in sunlight and the scent of salty air

PHOTOGRAPHY SHARYN CAIRNS

PREVIOUS PAGE With a view to the sea, our old cottage with bright yellow shutters and sandstone walls captures the morning light. **ABOVE** My husband, Dave, and I favour a relaxed, laid-back style. We have retained the narrative of the original cottage and the overall visual impact is of a timeless home, a true classic. The sunshine-yellow shutters make the home vibrate with a happy vibe. All paintings are by artist Susan Rothwell (Dave's mum), the shell sculpture is a Bali memento, while the cushions are from Perryman Carpets, Woollahra, NSW. The pendant is one of Dave's old craypots repurposed as a piece of coastal cool - he's a mad fisherman.

— — —

SARAH & DAVE ROTHWELL

Mother & property developer

WE HAD BEEN LOOKING FOR a home in a nearby suburb, but Dave was determined to be closer to the waves. We decided to drive past this place, which his parents had owned some years before, "just to look", as it was ultimately marked for subdivision and knockdown. But we instantly fell in love with what I can only describe as a piece of paradise, a magical yellow-and-white cottage perched high on the cliff, northeast facing and with expansive beach and ocean views.

The cottage, in Whale Beach, NSW, was rundown and the garden even more so, but this only inspired us more. We knew we could give it our special touch while preserving it at the same time. The yellow shutters against the white weatherboard and sandstone facade appealed to both of us enormously - they were here when we arrived and we have never considered changing them. Local builders had been living in the house and had converted the living room into a skate ramp! The cottage was truly ramshackle, but it had enormous potential and so much charm. There was nothing false about it.

We had both spent our childhoods in the country, so the feeling of space and greenery was a huge drawcard and, for the first time, I felt like this was the best of all worlds. The city is close enough for work, play and extended interests. The beach is a stroll away for surfing and swimming, and the cottage is set within a large garden, giving it a country feel. We decided it really was our dream place and somewhere we would be proud to call home and ultimately bring up children in. The only problem was it was soon to be a site for someone else's dream home!

To cut a long story short, the deal fell over, so we jumped at the chance to move in. Taps were falling off in the bathroom, the kitchen was almost unusable and needed a lot of work, but this was no deterrent. We bought the property and began planning a modest renovation. When we set about our renovations, it was quite a straightforward process, as we wanted to keep the house simple and beachy, and add layers with colour and texture. Cushions, art and rugs were selected to offset the otherwise neutral tones of the white walls, limewashed wooden floorboards and cream linen sofa covers.

...continued on page 108

OPPOSITE A collection of kitchen utensils and Corso De' Fiori jugs hangs on a rail for easy access. The little paintings are by Belle Black (on shelf) and my mother-in-law, Susan Rothwell (on bench). The kitchen bench is Carrara marble and the pendants are goatskin.

I LOVE
YOU ALL

...continued from page 105

There is a tribal element within the living area, with many of the pieces that cram our shelves and any flat surface collected as mementos from our holidays or as one-offs from auctions, which are always fun and great for a bargain.

The kitchen is open plan and absolutely the central social room in the house. Everyone in our family and extended family is adventurous in the kitchen and cooking plays a very important role in our family. The hanging pots were essential aesthetically and practically, and the perfectly positioned chalkboard on the side of the pantry and near the front door is for play, reminders and shopping lists. We cut out a barn door in the kitchen to help shield the room from the wind, but also to allow airflow and bring that big blue view inside while cooking - and, of course, as a nod to a family passion, horses. At one point, we had a Shetland pony named Popcorn living in the garden and we found it highly amusing when he would pop his head over the barn door and then walk straight through into the living room.

We have raised our three beautiful children, Lola, Florence and Monty, here from birth. Watching them collect the eggs from the chooks, pick fresh produce from the vegie garden, get up close and personal with water dragons and blue-tongue lizards and bask in the sun with Bear, our Burmese cat - and, for many years previously, Shumba, our blue Great Dane - are all precious moments that both Dave and I feel incredibly grateful for.

PREVIOUS PAGE The sandstone fireplace, goatskin pendants and a wall of unscripted bookshelves, stacked haphazardly with books and family holiday shots, are the heroes of this inviting room. The fireplace was rebuilt in the same position with old fenceposts found on the property. The wide timber floors were limewashed for a relaxed beach feel and the linen Jardan sofas are made extra comfy with muted earthy toned cushions from Perryman Carpets. Bar stools from Coco Republic.

TOP ROW The sun-kissed house with half doors and shutters painted in Dulux Sunburst yellow; my son, Monty's, cheeky shortcut to the kitchen; beautiful detail of two paint-splattered Egyptian pots – we bought a whole crate at auction. **MIDDLE ROW** Zebra skin drum coffee table from Seasonal Concepts, Redfern, NSW, teamed with Tom Dixon Form brass bowls and a pink succulent in terracotta pot; the charmingly modest entrance belies the expansive blue view that awaits. **BOTTOM ROW** Egyptian pots, a pile of succulents and pops of yellow welcome you to the front door; the view down to Whale Beach and beyond; the Rothwell kids, including Florence (foreground), Monty and Lola.

We decided to drive past this place "just to look" as ultimately it was already marked as a subdivision and knockdown. We instantly fell in love with what I can only describe as a piece of paradise, a yellow and white cottage perched high on a cliff, north-east facing with expansive beach and ocean views. The cottage was rundown and the garden even more so. However, this only inspired us more, as we knew that we could put our touch on it while preserving it at the same time.

PREVIOUS PAGE The deck offers a view for dolphin and whale sighting. Directors chairs from Eco Outdoor, Brookvale, NSW, marble tabletop from Prego Marble & Granite Works, with wrought-iron base bought at auction. Coffee table from Manyara Home, Mosman, NSW. Dave's craypots have been repurposed into pendants and we found the crazy mosaic pot on the console at auction. **ABOVE** Our bathroom is given a touch of whimsy befitting our fishing-mad family, with Cole & Son Fornasetti Acquario wallpaper. **OPPOSITE** Linen pendants from Les Interieurs, Newport, NSW, hang bedside. Bedouin Societe linen and Beach Road pink throw. Mirror bought at auction.

MIMM'S SHELTER

A cosy, much-coveted cottage has hugged the shoreline for more than a century

PHOTOGRAPHY SHARYN CAIRNS

MEL HAYHOE

Surfboard manufacturer

"MIMM'S COTTAGE." This is my name for our home in North Avalon, NSW, an acronym for its series of owners over its long life, Madge, Ian and Mayvis Breckridge, then me, Mel. Its original owners and builders were early generations of the Breckenridge family, who bought the land in 1913 to build a fisherman's cottage. They were timber merchants, hence the beautiful timber inside. Mayvis still lives next door, an inspiring 94 year old with so many stories of the home and the local area and the most incredible memory. I never tire of the stories – I could listen forever.

I met Mayvis some years ago, after popping a letter in her letterbox to see if she would be interested in renting us the cottage. To my excitement, she said yes. I signed the lease without even stepping inside – I thought, how bad could it be? It was a bit of a shock when I walked in. The previous tenants, who had kept rabbits inside, had not taken care of the cottage the way she deserved. I looked out the window to the view, took in the wooden panels throughout the house, then went into the little sunroom and thought, "This is going to be more than perfect". I spent a month fixing her up with my friend, Inez, and a gang of other helpers. We painted and cleaned, and had a load of fun in between – I even tiled the floor in my ensuite bathroom. After we rented it for a few years, Mayvis offered to let us buy the cottage, under the condition that we would never pull it down. We signed immediately. I, too, have stipulated that, when I pass it on, it cannot be demolished – these homes are precious and seldom found.

The 1913 fishing cottage is now my dining and sitting room, my absolute favourite place in the house. The timber walls are the original walls, as are the scruffy white timber floors. I could sit here and watch the ocean for hours, and I do! It's amazing in summer – with the bifold doors open, your eye travels from

...continued on page 130

PREVIOUS PAGE My sublime living room enjoys a view out to the ocean, framed by pine trees. Original timber panelled walls make for a unique space. The old sideboard and record player from another era team well with my recent splurge, two Børge Mogensen 1958 Spanish chairs. **OPPOSITE** The door off the sunroom trimmed in aqua. The boat against the pine was a gift from my late father. It's perfect filled with ice, champagne and beer. Not sure it was meant for that? **FOLLOWING PAGE** The original verandah, enclosed to create a suntrap, the ideal spot in the mornings with the sunrise lighting up the room, with that original mint green on the ceiling. Cushions a mix from Pony Rider and Society of Wanderers. A Barsony retro figurine on the cane coffee table. Fabric covering the daybed from Mark Tuckey. Timber fish from Beachwood, Avalon, NSW, and the old fishing rod belonged to my dad.

John

PREVIOUS PAGE So much to love in this room. The dining table and chairs were found on eBay - we painted the table top white and had the chairs restored and covered in Bruce Goold fabric. Mark Tuckey zigzag side table and a recent splurge, the vintage Børge Mogensen Spanish chairs, the comfiest chairs I've ever sat in. The palm tree artwork was a gift from my nephew, Ellis, the round palm tree tile is from Ahoy Traders and my absolute favourite is the drawing of a woman holding a snake by Cait Wait, an eBay find. **OPPOSITE** Plastic soldier bowl on the wall from a trip to Japan, while handmade shell curtains in the bedroom add to the coastal feel and the sheepskin makes this chair irresistible. Bedlinen from Deiji Studios. The woven bag on wall was a gift from my best friend, Rachel, brought back from Noumea. **FOLLOWING PAGE** Nearly everything in the living room was from eBay, including the mid-century Barsony table lamp and ashtray, the vintage sidetable, record player, porthole mirror and the Hawaiian girl print on the wall.

The original "Fishing Cottage" that was built in 1913 is now my dining & sitting room, my favourite place in the house. The original timber walls with scruffy white timber floors – I could sit & watch the ocean for hours on end – (and I do) x

SCRABBLE

4

ABOVE Last man standing on North Avalon, this fisherman's cottage will be here forever, thanks to me and Mayvis. The approach to the fisherman's cottage is past an electricity pole that I painted black and white, which strangely makes it kind of cool. Down the winding stone pathway and before you even approach the front door, your breath is literally taken away by the rush of ocean air. **OPPOSITE** Pineapple tile print from Ahoy Trader. Vintage petrol station number 4 from eBay (four is my favourite number). The hat and shells recall a holiday in Fiji.

...continued from page 119
the green grass to the rocks and across the ocean. The light, the smell of salt and the views pass through the cottage, triggering all the senses. A friend says this view, framed by pine trees, is the world's best television!

The sunroom, a cosy winter spot, is another favourite. Originally, it was the verandah, so there is a slight slope in the floor. We used the exterior of the house as the internal walls and found some old original windows on the property to enclose it. I have painted the walls white and the ceiling has always been this beautiful mint colour. I have never been able to find the exact colour, so I have left it exactly as it is, even with the paint peeling slightly. I find perfection boring – I love windows that rattle in the wind and screen doors that bang, the little quirky things that make my home feel warm and homely.

There are many favourite things in my home, with most collected from council clean-ups. I would go on my early morning walk, find so many great things, hide them in the bushes, and run home to grab the car and load up. One of my favourite finds is the vintage work bench under my kitchen window, perfect for the space. The day I found it, it was pouring with rain and I fetched my neighbour to help me carry it, as it weighed a tonne. We hauled it down to my place and I gave it some TLC with bees' wax. The top has a sunken shelf and I had a glass top made – we've filled it with our discarded oyster shells. All the pieces I have found have a tale to tell.

There are so many stories, like the original safe, weighing around 150g, that belonged to the Breckenridge family, which I would love to move into the kitchen and have on display, and one day I want to restore the original fireplace. Most of the stones that make the long boundary walls and the stepping stones in the entry have been brought up from the beach over time.

I love art with an Australiana feel. I have a few pieces from local artist Libby Watkins – I love her colours and I'm always a sucker for a hit of fluoro – but my favourite is the drawing by Cait Wait of an Aboriginal woman and her daughter, which I found in a garage sale for $50!

My other passion is cooking. Having moved out of home at 15, I had to learn quickly or starve. My kitchen is cluttered with things I love to cook with. When my new stove was being delivered, I had to paint the kitchen wall before it arrived and I had about eight hours to paint and allow it time to dry. I raced to the paint store to choose a colour, thinking I'd paint it black, but then a colour called aubergine caught my eye and what a fitting colour name for my kitchen.

My favourite surfing spot was always North Avalon. Sitting out in the water and looking across at my home always put a smile on my face. I don't surf often these days, but I love to swim any time of year. I always seem to pick the coldest day for a dip, then head home for a hot outdoor shower – you never regret a swim.

My home is my dream. As they say, home is where love resides, memories are created, friends and family always belong and the laughter never ends. Home is the place you want to return over and over and over again.

OPPOSITE The kitchen bench that I found on a council clean-up day. Old Man's Canggu print by Drew Wellman and all the crockery handmade by Jo Norton, Norton & Norton, Currumbin, Qld.
FOLLOWING PAGES A spot to hang your hat, keys and shopping bags, with mirror from Vinnies and palm print wallpaper from Kawaiian Lion; ceramic mid-century Barsony table lamp and ashtray – I've collected a few Barsony pieces. Love them – it's that glossy, yet matt-black, beachy vibe, which makes me smile; at my happiest, contemplating an early morning surf or will it be a swim?

OLD MAN'S
CANGGU
itsu the cookbook

4

27016

PALMY

Welcome inside a perfectly imperfect beauty,
an old salt with tales to tell

PHOTOGRAPHY SHARYN CAIRNS

— — —

SIOBHAN & WILL ROTHWELL

Interior designer and property developer

OUR 1920S COTTAGE COVERED IN RAMBLING VINES is nestled high on a hill, tucked among palm trees with a view across Pittwater, NSW, to Lion Island. It's magical. When we first found it, it was like stumbling upon a hidden treasure. While it's a little hike to get there, that makes it all the more worthwhile when you arrive. The minute I set foot on the meandering path bordered with tall bamboo, camellia and hibiscus bushes, I get an instant sensation of summer. Perhaps it's the overgrown vegetation and the sound of the ocean a short walk down the road that trigger all the emotions. We've strung lights up the path, which heightens the anticipation of all that awaits once we reach the top.

The cottage was built in the traditional Arts and Crafts style of the area and we gave it a sympathetic renovation a few years ago, restoring a lot of its original features and stripping away random '70s additions. I wanted to keep the nostalgic feel and respect the original cottage by not renovating it too much. We installed a new kitchen and bathroom, without changing their position or scale, and replaced the rotting timber floors, painting the new boards white for a casual vibe. With their high ceilings and generous floor areas, the proportions of each room are absolutely perfect and, because the cottage was crafted to such a good design, refurbishing the interiors was a sheer joy. I've worked on several period homes and, with this cottage, I've kept the interior relaxed and comfortable by using a neutral palette and adding interest through layers, texture and contemporary art. The next task for us is the exterior. While the roof doesn't leak, the walls need a bit of TLC and all the eaves need repair. Otherwise, she is in quite good shape.

What we first fell head over heels in love with were the massive stone fireplaces in the both living room and bedroom, which seemed so indulgent and romantic. There's also an artist's studio on the property, a gorgeous two-storey sandstone building, which we converted into a fourth bedroom. Plus I couldn't

...continued on page 154

PREVIOUS PAGE Could a room be more romantic than the bedroom, with its massive stone fireplace and enormous bay window, and the softest pink vintage rug and bedspread, both from Bali. All cushions on the bed were from Sally Campbell Handmade Textiles. **OPPOSITE** The perfect spot in the living room bay window, piled with cushions from Beachwood, Avalon, NSW, and Sally Campbell. The amber glass wall light is bespoke – the ivy, too, has found a way in.

PREVIOUS PAGE We bought the marble coffee table, comfy linen sofa and chalky white table lamp from MCM House, Paddington, NSW. Our cushions in the bay window are a mix from Beachwood and Sally Campbell Handmade Textiles. Ceramics on coffee table were from Mud, Mosman, NSW, and Dunlin, Paddington, NSW. **OPPOSITE** I chose a Carrara marble kitchen benchtop and splashback, and then kept it relaxed with blond timber bar stools and a custom console from Bali. Ceramics by Georgie Dolling, basket from Beachwood and 'Beach Bums' photographic print by Akila Berjaoui.

TOP ROW A two-storey stone artist's studio was the first building on the property; sunlight streams through the bedroom's bay window, with Tonk stool from MCM House and raffia cushion from Water Tiger, St Peters, NSW; an outdoor bath on the back deck, ideal for moonlit soaks. Wooden pot, stool and candlestick, all from Water Tiger. Judd stool, MCM House, and Saardé towels, Montmartre Store, Mosman, NSW. **MIDDLE ROW** Cosy bedroom in the artist's studio, with kantha embroidered quilt from Sally Campbell Handmade Textiles, cushions from Beachwood and ceramics from Dunlin. **BOTTOM ROW** Beauty of a moss detail; model boat on mantel; outdoor furniture by Rothwell Design, made to order, cushions from Montmartre Store.

ABOVE AND PREVIOUS PAGE The living room is made for barefoot nonchalance, where nothing is too precious. The black-and-white photographic print, 'Ibiza' by Ross Lawrence, anchors the space. **OPPOSITE** The western deck and its beautiful stone chimney stack. **FOLLOWING PAGE** You have to try bathing outdoors in the dead of night, summer or winter, at least once in your life. Saardé towels from Montmartre Store and linen shower screen from Bibbithings.

Kick off the shoes, open up the house nestled
among the trees, the gentle breeze rustles the
leaves & comes in through the house, shells
tinkle, & water shimmers in the distance.
All evocative of summer holidays!

…continued from page 141
resist adding an outdoor bath and shower to the deck. We also built a new deck to the western side of the property and I designed the lightweight timber modular outdoor seating pieces outside. We spend a lot of time out here. There is also a little stone turret, a wonderful folly that attracts lots of comments, with an outdoor fire surrounded with old tree stumps for seating. Something about a fire makes you gather and talk – the kids, Mia, 10; Oliver, eight; Sebastian, six; and Sasha, three, all love this special spot.

Adding to the building's curiosities and charms is the Romeo and Juliet sandstone balcony off the patio – it's romantically smothered in vines, which I left intact. That covered patio is another entertaining area, with a mother-of-pearl chandelier that tinkles in the wind and adds to the sensory experience of holidays. We found that light fitting and the rattan dining setting beneath it in Bali. I love the original blue ceiling in the space, which, although I was tempted to paint white, I decided to leave just as it was, true to the spirit of the original home – and it makes me smile.

Other gathering places in the cottage are the two huge bay windows, one in the bedroom with its linen oatmeal curtains, a sunny spot where the kids often drag a pile of cushions. The living room has a custom-made seat in the bay window, which is piled with cushions in all shapes and sizes for lazy family days.

I couldn't imagine a more perfect holiday home for all our family and friends. Our secret escape, it's a home away from home, which is all heart and nourishes the soul.

PREVIOUS PAGE The summer verandah, with its quirky blue ceiling, rattan chairs, marble tabletop and mother-of-pearl chandelier – it's a room from yesterday but at the same time very much now. Everything is bespoke, except the chandelier, which I brought back from Bali. **OPPOSITE** The stone turret is the perfect place for our fire pit. Happy days – and nights!

CRAIGIE LEE

A much-loved bush bungalow, perched
on a hill overlooking the Pacific

PHOTOGRAPHY FELIX FOREST

Aloha

PREVIOUS PAGE The perfectly pitched roofline and an exterior clad in timber from crates originally used to ship cars. Timber painted in Palm Beach Black timber stain from Porter's Paints. **ABOVE** We, Sarah and Jeff, are the Darling Blairs, co-founders of Map of the Heart, an iconic fragrance line, while Jeff is also a filmmaker. Together we have four beautiful, creative kids, all grown up now - Scout, Cooper, Imogen and Carson. Garden painting to the left by David McKay, from the Lone Goat Gallery, Byron Bay, NSW, while the painting on right is of Cooper, painted by Scout, at age 11. The cloud photograph is by Michael Kenna. **FOLLOWING PAGE** The intensity of the black adds theatre to the simplicity of wattle on the mantel. Magnetic sculpture by Mikala Dwyer. Vase a secondhand find.

— — —

SARAH BLAIR & JEFF DARLING

Co-founders of a fragrance company and filmmaker

THE FIRST TIME I saw Craigie Lee, at Palm Beach, NSW, was when Jeff used it as a location. I don't think we even went inside, as we were only able to use the outside. But I was immediately enchanted by it and the fact that something so unsuburban could still exist. Over the years, we would occasionally walk by it and see it always empty. We then had another house on an adjacent hill, which had great bones but had been added to badly. It was on three blocks of land, with fruit trees, a vegetable garden and lawns for the kids to run riot on. Jeff would skateboard down the sweeping stone driveway, with one of the kids holding onto him and screaming with the sheer thrill, until they spilled onto the lawn.

Then we got to thinking about taking the soul of that house and making it into what it could be in this bungalow on the other hill – we especially loved the generous verandah. Then, one day in late January, an auction sign appeared at the gate. The old house, with its holes in the verandah and water-swollen Masonite walls where it had been closed in, was for sale, together with all its original furniture and, even better, the block next to it.

We weren't looking to move, but a house like this gets under your skin. We had sold our company and, the day before the auction, the money hit the account. The night before the auction, I went up and sat on the verandah, because we didn't know what to do. We had not long moved, which had been such a lot of work – but then the full moon rose up over the ocean and the salt air filled my nostrils, and I was gone. I said to the wind and the moon, "Don't do this to me". But it was too late. This falling-down house just sang to us. And still we didn't know what to do. The next day, Jeff had to go into town and rang when he was driving, saying he was going to the auction, because, at the very least, he had to know what it went for.

...continued on page 181

OPPOSITE The deep verandah with its view through the eucalyptus trees to the Pacific Ocean. **FOLLOWING PAGES** The kind of home that evokes memories, Craigie Lee has an aura of summer holidays. John Fielding of Bellevarde Constructions used carpenters to rebuild the rumble verandah wall, because I didn't want it perfect and a stonemason would have found that too tempting; it's a very personal home, with items that hold memory and history. A very English rug, by Vivienne Westwood for The Rug Company, makes a statement in the living room, complete with a Robert Moore painting and a Michael Kenna framed photograph on the wall. Colourful cushions made from Chee Soon and Fitzgerald fabric.

Sunrise Road

Everytime I go there, I step out of the car and let a long breath out.

It's solitariness, secret sense makes me feel safe. I like its hardness, its sense that it was a place to take the air and feel robust and healthy. I see lots of rosy cheeks and thick woollen jumpers.

I would love to offer our children a poetic kind of life there. Spaces to paint and draw and make a mess, to do woodworking – to be able to take apart an engine. Spaces to sit and read in or out of the sun, to listen to the waves. To walk around and feel water all around like an island. To be more connected to the beach, to walk down to the park, to the ferry. To set us on a path of a different kind of family.

It is

TOP ROW Dining room with painting by Jasper Knight; the back door to the little guest bedroom; a spot for wetsuit storage under the house. **MIDDLE ROW** Foraged, heart-shaped beach pebbles and ocean-worn glass; windows with frosted glass and poppies in the light. **BOTTOM ROW** A cupboard full of colourful rugs crocheted by Jeff's mum; a painting in the narrow hallway, by Stephen Marr, leads towards a classic Eames chair; a stairway in the new tall house, designed by architect Rob Brown, looks like it's been there forever. Artworks by the kids and Heather Blair. **OPPOSITE** Cow painting by Robert Moore, lamp a second-hand find and cushions made with fabric sourced from Chee Soon and Fitzgerald.

R. Moore. 90

OPPOSITE We hunted out linoleum kitchen tiles as close as possible to the originals and installed an Aga stove and long stainless-steel benchtop. The vegies are kept in an original trapdoor in the floor. **FOLLOWING PAGES** A view into the bush from the deep verandah. I found the armchairs by the side of the road and had them recovered. The string of coloured lighting makes for a charming scene at night. Plump cushions add colour and pattern; a vintage bed and a metal desk in Scout's bedroom complement the wonderful period oak panelling.

MORTON
SALT

FUTURE TECH
ORSON SCOTT CARD
ENDER'S GAME
DAVE EGGERS
TO KILL A Mockingbird
PETER PAN
THE HOLE BOOK
HOW THINGS WORK
WARPLANES
SCULPTING A GALAXY
HUMAN ANATOMY
FOR ARTISTS
THE ARRIVAL
SHAUN TAN
organic Don Burke
ORGANIC GARDENING PETER BENNETT
STENCIL REPUBLIC
TJANPI DESERT WEAVERS

REINHART
STAR WARS
A GALACTIC POP-UP ADVENTURE
MAGICAL CREATURES HANDBOOK
GEARS OF WAR
SHADOWRUN

TOP ROW Books, books and more books in the library; the open dish rack came with the house; a vintage first-aid box in the bathroom, packed with essentials. **MIDDLE ROW** The bathroom cabinet, an original from the house; a dream pink Eames Shell chair on wheels looks a picture against a wall of books. **BOTTOM ROW** A bedroom with quilts from Sally Campbell; the fireplace needed revamping, so we set about deconstructing it stone by stone, then rebuilding it to last another 100 years; we reinstalled the water tanks to harvest rainwater for the garden. **OPPOSITE** The original bath features repurposed garden taps. **FOLLOWING PAGE** Architect Rob Brown's tall house complements the original house perfectly.

...continued from page 163

It was passed in and then he met with the family, who remembered him from shooting there. They knew he loved it and wouldn't pull it down, and would keep the land with it. So we bought it. The two old ladies in their 90s that we bought it from had holidayed there as children. It had been in the family since the 1930s and it wasn't just about the money - it was about finding someone who loved it. This hill used to be called Spin Hill, because it was where spinsters had their homes and the other hill in Palm Beach was called Pill Hill, because that was where the doctors had their weekenders. This had always been a holiday house and no-one had lived in it full-time - with the exception of a possum that lived permanently in the cupboard!

The bungalow, designed by James Peddle of Peddle and Thorp (later Peddle Thorp & Walker) in 1914, was influenced by the US Arts and Crafts movement. It had great bones, but we were unsure what to do with it and it needed so much work. So we came from the other hill and camped on the weekends. But, when we moved in for one summer, there was no turning back. We found our architect, Rob Brown of Casey Brown Architecture, from a similar house he had down the road. I'll never forget the first drawing he did for his original presentation. It was a water colour of the sun's path and so delicate. He spent the day smelling the breeze and feeling the sun.

The renovation was about keeping the integrity of the original bungalow. But we also wanted a house that was large enough to accommodate us all as our full-time home, and where it was okay to jump on the furniture and, if the kids were painting and got paint on something, it wasn't a disaster.

Rob designed a two-storey pavilion separate from the original house, modern in scale and with larger windows, not small paned as in the old cottage. It took a year to design and a year to build and was awarded the 2002 RAIA Francis Greenway State Award and the 2002 RAIA Lachlan Macquarie National Award. While the two buildings speak to each other materially, there was never any attempt to copy the old house in the new. The long room, with its sliding wall/door that looks into the bush is where we hang in the daytime if we are not on the verandah and where projects are worked on. Our bedroom on top of the tall building - with windows on four sides, is heavenly, a cubby for adults removed from the rest of the house.

As the kids grew up, they put on shows in the long room. They painted, they sewed, built things, drew, made films, cooked, ran riot, cooked marshmallows on the fire, watched films on the outdoor screen and walked to the beach and back to swim and surf. If it was cold in winter, we would all wear jumpers and feel it. In the summer, there was usually a cool breeze, but there was always a spot to be found in the sun or shade. When you walk between the buildings and it is raining, you get wet. You feel the sun, smell the salt or see the moon rise above the sea.

The old house constantly surprises me. All these years later, I glimpse something I've not noticed before. Nothing is straight, there is no framing and the walls are Oregon from crates that cars were once shipped in. The rubble-stone walls and fireplace are from stone found locally. Scale is a little topsy turvy, but I love the fireplace that's too big for the room and the little rooms that throw you outside, unless the weather is inclement - then you bunker in, safe and sound. The covered verandah, again very large for the house, is where we live. We eat every meal we can out there and all our friends know to bring jumpers to dinner.

Every single day we feel lucky to live here. It's a sanctuary and feels so much of who we all are.

ABOVE Our bedroom perched up in the trees. We found the bedside reading lights in New York. **OPPOSITE** The library with retro chairs from Spence & Lyda, Surry Hills, NSW, and Roy Lichtenstein 'Oh Jeff, I Love You' cushions from the Tate Modern. A film case has been repurposed as a coffee table. **FOLLOWING PAGE** Old stackable Sebel chairs on the terrace, a vintage find.

— — —

RESOURCES

Insider info and tips from the homeowners to help you achieve your own unique interior style

THE LITTLE BLACK SHACK

You can stay at The Little Black Shack. Go to thelittleblackshack.com.au, @thelittleblackshack.

PAINT

Porter's Paints
W porterspaints.com
P 1800 656 664
E enquiries@porters.com.au
I @porterspaints
Half wall painted in Porter's Blue Black environmentally friendly low VOC.

VINTAGE FINDS

Antique General Store
W antiquegeneralstore.com
P (02) 9913 7636
I @antiquegeneralstore

Lunatiques
W lunatiques.com
P 0488 043 232
E @lunatiques
Vintage finds galore, especially those with a pre-loved patina.

Mockingbird Lane Antiques
tilbaantiques.com.au
P (02) 4473 7226
E info@mockingbirdlane antiques.com

Elements
W elements.net.au
P (02) 9560 3067
E mail@elements.net.au
I @elements_i_love

Eclectic Find
W eclecticfind.com.au
P 0414 502 348
E eclecticfind1@gmail.com
I @electicfind

LINEN

Ici et Là
W icietla.com.au
P 0481 533 284
I @icietla

In Bed
W inbedstore.com
P (02) 9358 4245
E info@inbedstore.com
I @inbedstore
We use only high quality, natural fibres and fabrics, always ensuring with our producers that ethical practices are maintained.

LIGHTING

Edison Light Globes
W edisonlightglobes.com
P (03) 9396 1421
E support@edisonlightglobes.com.au
I @edisonlightglobes

HARDWARE

Bunnings
W bunnings.com.au
P (03) 8831 9777
I @bunnings
Garden taps, barn door locks, you name it!

ART

Ingrid Kwong
Little Scapes
W littlescapesart.com
P 0400 515 588
E littlescapesart@gmail.com
I @littlescapes

Mick Mock
P 0403 974 967
Vintage paintings and surf memorabilia.

Nikki Bridger
Nikki B's store
F facebook.com/pages/category/Gift-Shop/Nikki-Bs-1557418247827116/
P (02) 4454 5661
Artist.

Linda Barrip
W desiredharmony.com
P 0402 114 940
E desiredharmony@gmail.com
I @desiredharmony

TIP: Black stain on timber exterior and interior is a mix of Palm Beach Black water-based stain by Porter's Paints and a custom brown Porter's Paints tint to warm up the colour.

WATERVIEW

ART

Julia Ritson
W juliaritson.com
P 0449 982 194
E julia@juliaritson.com
I @juliaritson

Sophie Gannon Gallery
W sophiegannongallery.com.au/artists/philip-hunter
P (03) 9421 0857
E info@sophiegannongallery.com.au
I @sophiegannongallery

PAINT

W dulux.com.au
P 13 25 25
E dulux.customer.service@dulux.com.au
I @duluxaus
Paint colours we used: Algae; Linseed; Leaf Tea.

TILES

Artedomus
W artedomus.com
P 1300 278 338
E sales@artedomus.com
I @artedomus

TEXTILES

Burel (Portugal)
W burelfactory.com
P +351 913 285 370
E isabel.costa@burelfactory.com

Maku Textiles
E info@makutextiles.com
I @makutextiles

FURNITURE

Patricia Urquiola (Living Edge)
W livingedge.com.au
P 1300 132 154
E info@livingedge.com.au
I @livingedge

Hans Wegner (Cult)
W cultdesign.com.au
P 1300 768 626
E info@cultdesign.com.au
I @cultdesignau

Ercol (UK)
W ercol.com
P +44 (0)1844 271839
E international.sales@ercol.com
@ecolfurniture

GYPSY CREEK

You can stay at Gypsy Creek. Go to louellawhatever.com.

PAINT

Dulux
(See Waterview)
Front door and all bathrooms in Classic Calm low VOC All Weather low sheen.

Taubmans
W taubmans.com.au
T 131 686
E info@taubmans.com.au
I @taubmans

White Knight
W whiteknightpaints.com.au
P 13 16 86
E info@whiteknightpaints.com.au
I @whiteknightpaints
All the floors in Classic White White Knight paving paint.

Porter's Paints
(See The Little Black Shack)

Rockcote
W rockcote.com.au
P 1300 736 668
Walls in Rockote water-based Ecostyle non-toxic low VOC to match Porter's Paints Popcorn.

LIGHTING

The Society Inc
W thesocietyinc.com.au
P (02) 9516 5643
E hello@thesocietyinc.com.au
I @sibellacourt

BASINS

Slab Shapers
W slabshapers.com
P 0447 752 060
E slabshapers@gmail.com
I @slabshapers

RUGS

Loom Rugs
W loomrugs.com
P (03) 9510 3040
E loom@loomrugs.com
I @loomrugs

NSW Leather Co.
W leatherco.com.au
P (02) 9355 3600
E nswl@leatherco.com.au
I @nsw _ leather _ co
Sheepskins and cowhide rugs.

HARDWARE

Normann Copenhagen
(HG Furniture Solutions)
W hgfs.com.au/normann-copenhagen
P (02) 9693 2288
I @hgfurnituresolutions
Stone handles.

Bunnings
(See Little Black Shack)

The Society Inc.
(See previous column)
Great hooks for hanging things.

FURNITURE

Leonard Joel
W leonardjoel.com.au
P (03) 9826 4333
E info@leonardjoel.com.au
I @leonardjoelauctions
Borge Møgensen Spanish chairs.

Maker & Son
W makerandson.com.au
P 0452 549 371
I @makerandson
White armchairs are 'The most comfortable armchairs in the world'. Business based in Sussex, UK, but also manufactures in Melbourne, Portland (US), and Florence (Italy). Sustainable and eco-aware company.

Louella Whatever
W louellawhatever.com
P 0412 878 966
E louellawhatever@gmail.com
I @louellaboitelgill
Timber beds, sofas, kitchen benchtops, designed by Louella Whatever, made to order at the Mark Tuckey workshop in Melbourne.

Greg Hatton
W greghatton.com
P 0411 624 712
E emailme@greghatton.com
I @greghatton
Twiggy table made to order.

ART

Mitcham Antique Gallery
P (08) 8272 9363

Vintage Posters Only
W vintagepostersonly.com
P (03) 9500 2505
E sam@vintagepostersonly.com
I @vintageposters
Vintage poster a gift from friend Sam Johnson in Melbourne.

The Society Inc.
(See previous column)
Oversized safety pin.

TILES

Jatana Tiles
W jatanainteriors.com.au
P (02) 6688 4235
E info@jatanainteriors.com.au
I @jatanainteriors
Huge selection of incredibly unusual tiles.

LINEN

The Society of Wanderers
W societyofwanderers.com
P (03) 5209 2564
E hello@societyofwanderers.com
I @societyofwanderers
Floral quilts and striped sheets.

Pony Rider
W ponyrider.com.au
P (02) 8911 3518
E info@ponyrider.com.au
I @pony _ rider
Organic cotton duvet covers and pillowcases.

Castle
W castleandthings.com.au
P 0403 854 758
E hello@castleandthings.com.au
I @rachelcastleandthings
Rach has the best linen and I always use her tea towels as art - they're too beautiful for drying dishes.

TIP: Timber benches can be a pain if water sits on the benchtop without being wiped. The bench will stain and eventually get mould. With this secret recipe, it will be safe: waterproof with Sherwin-Williams Croma Coatings Clear Matt 2K UV Prohibitor Waterborne Hardener. Three coats all round and you're good to go.

MIMM'S SHELTER

FURNITURE

Angelucci Vintage
W angelucci.net.au
P (03) 9415 8001
E fitzroy@angelucci.net.au
I @angelucci20thcentury

Mark Tuckey
W marktuckey.com.au
P (03) 9419 3418
E fitzroy@marktuckey.com.au
I @mark _ tuckey

ART

Deus Customs (Deus Ex Machina)
W deuscustoms.com
P (02) 8594 2800
E eshop@deuscustoms.com
I @deuscustoms

Ahoy Trader
W ahoytrader.com
E customerservice@ahoytrader.com
I @ahoytrader
Tile art.

Bruce Goold
W brucegoold.com
E brucegoold@aapt.net.au
I @brucegooldartist

CERAMICS

Jo Norton
Thrown By Jo
W thrownbyjo.com
E jo@thrownbyjo.com
I @thrownbyjo

CUSHIONS & LINEN

Pony Rider
P (02) 8911 3518
E info@ponyrider.com.au
I @pony _ rider

Beachwood
W beachwood.com.au
P (02) 9918 7162
E us@beachwood.com.au
I @beachwooddesigns

Society of Wanderers
W societyofwanderers.com
P (03) 5209 2564
E hello@societyofwanderers.com
I @societyofwanderers
Best-kept secret for nostalgic linen.

Deiji Studios
W deijistudios.com.au
E info@deijistudios.com.au
I @deijistudios

WALLPAPER

W kawaiianlion.com
I @kawaian _ lion

RUGS

Worn
W wornstore.com.au
E hello@wornstore.com.au
I @worn.store
Sheepskin from this cool store.

PAINT

Dulux (see Waterview)
Kitchen paint colour is Dulux Aubergine.

VINTAGE FINDS

eBay
W ebay.com.au
I am a mad eBay shopper.

SURFBOARDS

Onboard store
W onboardstore.com.au
P (02) 9997 8266
I @onboard _ store
Surfboard from Chris Christenson, a pink C-Bucket Model.

TIP: Check out the local tip, such as in my area, the Kimbriki Buy Back Centre, kimbriki.com.au. Some tips have shops attached and you can seriously find some unique pieces that people have discarded, but are perfect for another life.

PALMY

PAINT

Porter's Paints
(see Little Black Shack)
My perfect white for the cottage is Porter's Paints Popcorn.

FABRIC

Unique Fabrics
W uniquefabrics.com
P (03) 9816 2000
I @unique _ fabrics

FURNITURE & LIGHTING

MCM House
W mcmhouse.com
P (02) 9358 0800
E info@mcmhouse.com
I @mcmhouse
Sofa and marble-top coffee table.

Dunlin
W dunlin.com.au
P 1800 649 586
E orders@dunlin.com.au
I @dunlinhome

Water Tiger
W watertiger.com.au
P 0420 855 886
I @ _ watertiger _

CUSHIONS & LINEN

Sally Campbell
Handmade Textiles
W sallycampbell.com.au
P 0415 403 760
E sallyruthcam@ozemail.com.au
I @sallycampbelltextiles

Montmartre Store
W montmartrestore.com.au
P (02) 9969 5456
I @montmartrestore

Beachwood
(see Mimm's Shelter)

Bibbithings
P 0412 241 572
I @bibbithings
Linen shower curtain

CERAMICS

Georgie Dolling
W georgiedolling.com
I @georgie _ dolling

SUNTRAP

AUCTION HOUSES

Leonard Joel
W leonardjoel.com.au
P (03) 9826 4333,
(02) 9362 9045
E info@leonardjoel.com.au
I @leonardjoelauctions

Lawsons
W lawsons.com.au
P (02) 9566 2377
E info@lawsons.com.au
I @lawsonauctioneers

CARPETS & CUSHIONS

Perryman Carpets
W perrymancarpets.com
P (02) 9327 3910
I @perrymancarpets

LIGHTING

Les Interieurs Studio
W lesinterieurs.com.au
P (02) 9999 6479
E pamela@lesinterieurs.com.au
I @lesinterieursnewport

PAINT

Dulux (see Waterview)
The yellow on all shutters and doors is Sunburst.

STONE AND GRANITE

Prego Marble & Granite Works
W pregoworks.com.au
P 0410 770 235
E pregomarble@gmail.com
I @pregomarbleandgranite
Chat to Rui Prego.

ART

Susan Rothwell from Justin Miller Art
W justinmillerart.com
P (02) 9331 7777
E info@justinmillerart.com
I @justinmillerart

FURNITURE

Jardan
W jardan.com.au
P (03) 8581 4999
E world@jardan.com.au
I @jardanfurniture

Manyara Home
W manyarahome.com.au
P (02) 9969 0137
E mosman@manyarahome.com.au
I @manyarahome
Marble-top coffee table.

Coco Republic
W cocorepublic.com.au
P 1300 000 220
I @cocorepublic
Bar stools.

OUTDOOR FURNITURE

Eco Outdoor
W ecooutdoor.com.au
P 1300 131 413
E info@ecooutdoor.com.au
I @ecooutdoor

LINEN

Bedouin
Fenton & Fenton
W fentonandfenton.com.au
P 1800 433 686
E hello@fentonandfenton.com.au
I @fenton _ and _ fenton

WALLPAPER

Cole & Son (UK)
Fornasetti Acquario
Seafoam wallpaper
W cole-and-son.com/en/collection-642/
P +44 (0)208 442 8844
E customer.service@cole-and-son.com
I @cole _ and _ son _ wallpapers

Steal the Limelight
W stealthelimelight.com.au
P (02) 9939 9836
E info@stealthelimelight.com.au
I @steal _ the _ limelight

THROW

Beachwood
(see Mimm's Shelter)
Note: The velvety pink throw has the softest sheepskin on the underside.

TIP: Best and most unique finds are always at the auction houses. Make sure you get on the mailing list for upcoming notifications so you don't miss out. They send through early catalogue items, so you can get a heads up.

CRAIGIE LEE

FURNITURE

Spence & Lyda
W spenceandlyda.com.au
P (02) 9212 6747
E mail@spenceandlyda.com.au
I @spenceandlyda

Herman Miller (Aust)
W hermanmiller.com
I @hermanmillerasia
Pink Eames chairs.

CUSHIONS

Chee Soon Fitzgerald
W cheesoonfitzgerald.com
P (02) 8399 1305
E contact@cheesoonfitzgerald.com

ART

Hamiltons (UK)
W hamiltonsgallery.com
P +44 207 499 9493
E art@hamiltonsgallery.com
I @hamiltonsgallery

Michael Kenna
W michaelkenna.net
I @michaelkennaphoto

HARDWARE

Johnson Brothers
W jbhmv.com.au
P (02) 9999 3340
I @thereal _ jbhmv

Bunnings (see Little Black Shack)

PAINT

Porter's Paints
(see Little Black Shack)
We used Palm Beach Black.

RUGS

The Rug Company (UK)
W therugcompany.com
P +44 203 369 3912
E customerserviceint@therugcompany.com
I @therugcompany

TIP: In the kitchen, we used linoleum instead of vinyl. It's made with all-natural plant materials and is biodegradable, versus vinyl, which is a man-made plastic - it's a no-brainer.

THANK YOU So many people give of their time, energy and love when you're creating a book and these are all the people that supported me and helped me push this passion project over the line.

My name is on the cover, but this book has truly been a collaboration with art director Andrea Healy, and photographers Sharyn Cairns and Felix Forest. I am eternally grateful to you all. I think that's kind of an IOU.

Sharyn Cairns, thank you for being my knight in shining armour, for seeing things differently, for your passion and integrity. Andrea Healy - since working in interior magazines, I have always wanted to work with you on a book, so thank you for saying yes - you are an exquisite craftswoman and a true visionary. Felix Forest, thank you for being part of the adventure - your shots are all emotion, heart and soul.

But this book is not images alone - my thanks to interiors writer and editor Chris Pearson, with your keen eye you have ensured the words are perfectly perfect. Thank you, John McDonald, for your huge heart and always having my back. Simone Aquilina for keeping us on track. Bauer Books general manager Sally Eagle for being inspired and signing us up - no book without you, Sal. Bauer Books for the beautiful production and Random House for getting us into all the bookshops. David Scotto for being our public relations whizz. Special thanks to stylist Hannah Brady for adding such a special touch to Palmy. Your eye is unique and your dedication to the task unfailing - climbing thousands of stairs with me and still laughing.

Georgie Campbell for sharing her love of the house on the ocean's edge, the one with the yellow shutters, and thank you for introducing me to the big-hearted Sarah and Dave Rothwell. Giselle Chadwick for sharing stories and possibilities. And my dear friend, Peter Stutchbury, for not hesitating when I asked if he'd write the foreword for the book - he has an extraordinary way of seeing and communicating. Plus, a big thanks to all the amazing home owners for sharing their gorgeous homes with us, allowing us to snoop around and then hound you for all your secret resources. Louella Boitel-Gill - Gypsy Creek is an incredible creation, you are a super talent. Sarah Blair and Jeff Darling - it finally happened! Thank you for your generosity, loyalty and patience, and especially for keeping your home under wraps for me - can't thank you enough. Ingrid and Jamie Kwong - The Little Black Shack is where I'd like to hang my hat one day, just saying. Sarah and Dave Rothwell - your home is the best kept secret in Whale Beach - thank you for saving it, literally. Mel Hayhoe - simply the best house in Avalon with the best designer armchairs. A true custodian of place. John Wardle - honoured to include you and the captain in this book - another level altogether. Siobhan and Will Rothwell - thank you for sharing this romantic dream tangled in vines. Shayne Allen - thank you for hooking me up with the glorious Palmy house. Your energy and passion for interiors always fires me up. I feel honoured to have worked with all these beautiful people.

Finally, thanks to my bestie, Claire, for the endless encouragement and to my beautiful family - mum, Jack, Alli and Lau for all the love and support.

Published 2020 by
Bauer Media Books

Bauer Media Pty Limited
54 Park Street, Sydney;
GPO Box 4088 Sydney,
NSW 2001 Australia
phone (+61) 2 8116 9334

Editor Deborah Bibby

Art direction Andrea Healy
Copy editor Chris Pearson
Photography © Sharyn Cairns
and © Felix Forest

Chief executive officer, Bauer Media
Brendon Hill

Chief financial officer, Bauer Media
Andrew Stedwell

Publisher, Bauer Media Books
Sally Eagle

International rights manager,
Bauer Media Books
Simone Aquilina
saquilina@bauer-media.com.au

Printed in China
by Leo Paper Products

A catalogue record for this book
is available from the
National Library of Australia

ISBN 978-1-92586-548-6

Bauer Media ABN 18 053 273 546

To order books, phone 13 61 16
(within Australia) or order online
at magshop.com.au

Deborah Bibby has 20+ years' experience leading teams across print, product and digital. Bibby was founding editor-in-chief of interiors magazine *Real Living*, has edited numerous titles in both Sydney and London, and was most recently founding editor-in-chief of *JONES* and *Mr.Jones* magazines. Bibby's passion lies in interiors, the more unscripted and unexpected the better. She is currently working on a new platform in the interior space.

Andrea Healy has been quietly transforming the page with her creative vision for more than 25 years on magazine and book titles across interiors, architecture, fashion and food, including *Real Living, Vogue, Vogue Living* and *Marie Claire Lifestyle*. Always understated and thoughtfully edited, her work seeks to reveal the essence of beautiful design. Healy is currently art director of *Real Living* magazine.

Sharyn Cairns is a photographer and creator of some of the most beautiful emotive images across interiors, food, travel and lifestyle. Cairns is known for her love of natural light – her imagery will have you captivated. Her work is featured in *Belle, Gourmet Traveller, Dwell, Kinfolk, Elle Decoration UK, Vogue Living* and many others. Cairns is currently working on a major photographic exhibition.

Felix Forest is a photographer and an artist with an eye for the narrative. His work has been described as "curious and poetic". Forest lives between Sydney and Paris and has shot for most international interiors magazines, including *AD Spain; Vogue Living; Elle Decoration UK*, to name a few. Forest is currently involved in a range of photographic exhibitions, portraits and mixed media.

———

PHOTOGRAPHY Sharyn Cairns: WATERVIEW pp46-75, GYPSY CREEK pp76-99, SUNTRAP pp100-115, MIMM'S SHELTER pp116-135, PALMY pp136-155, FRONT ENDPAPER, PORTRAIT p11, PORTRAIT p161
Felix Forest: COVER, FRONTISPIECE, CONTENTS, INTRODUCTION p6,
THE LITTLE BLACK SHACK pp8-45, CRAIGIE LEE pp156-185, p190, P192, BACK ENDPAPERS